WINNING Résumé

WINNING Résumé

How to write an impressive Curriculum Vitae (CV) that guarantees you an interview call

Jayant Neogy

UNICORN BOOKS

Publisher

UNICORN BOOKS

F-2/16, Ansari Road, Daryaganj, New Delhi-110002
☎ 011-23275434, 23262683, 23250704 • *Fax:* 011-23257790
E-mail: info@unicornbooks.in • *Website:* www.unicornbooks.in

Branch : Mumbai

23-25, Zaoba Wadi Thakurdwar, Mumbai-401002

☎ 022-22010941, 022-22053387

E-mail: rapidex@bom5.vsnl.net.in

Showroom :

★ **PM Publications,** New Delhi
- 10-B, Netaji Subhash Marg, Daryaganj
  New Delhi-110002
- 6686, Khari Baoli, Delhi-110006

Distributors :

★ **Pustak Mahal,** New Delhi

Delhi: ☎ 011-23276539

Bengaluru: ☎ 080-22234025

Patna: ☎ 0612-3294193

★ **V & S Publishers,** Hyderabad
☎ 040-24737290

ISBN 978-81-7806-032-3
Winning Resume (English)

Edition: 2012

Printed at : *Param Offsetters, Okhla, New Delhi-110020*

Best of luck in your job hunt!

—Jayant Neogy

Preface

Time was when the author himself was a tremulous and hopeful hunter in the job jungle. Much of the anxiety of those early and unsure days is still well remembered. I remember the sleepless nights and the sweaty palms. I remember the breathless wait for the postman, the trepidation that no interview call will ever materialise. I felt totally inadequate to showcase my professional capabilities in the written form, being trained primarily to solve differential equations and to draw third angle projections of a gearbox! I yearned for a good guidebook for writing job applications, but none was to be found. Someday, I thought, when I have the time, I will write a guidebook myself!

I am thankful to Dr. Ashok Gupta, MD, Unicorn books for his encouragement and help in giving concrete shape to that nebulous idea of long ago. My research showed that a résumé is really a subtly written piece of advertisement. Like all advertisements, it requires that the writer objectively understands the product, that is, himself, and the target audience, that is the potential employer. This insight made me look at the art of résumé writing from an entirely new angle.

This book is the result of that insight. It is for the fresh entrant to the field of job-hunting as much as it is for the veteran chief executive furthering his already illustrious career. There are many hints and tips here to stimulate your thought processes and cues to make you look at your skills and capabilities in an entirely new light. There are practical guidelines for crafting, arresting and visually pleasing résumés that will stand out amongst a thousand others. In short, it is a fully loaded toolbox for you to use as you produce your masterpiece of a résumé.

The Chapters

If you must post your résumé tomorrow, go through *"A Last Minute Guidebook" in Chapter 1 "Bag that Interview!"* Here you will find tips you can use immediately to polish what you have already written. It will put some pep in your profile.

However, to write an outstanding résumé, you will need to look at your achievements in a new light. To learn the latest tricks and techniques of how to research and prepare, read *Chapters 1 to 4.* Then, to write out your masterpiece, read *Chapter 5, "Nuts and Bolts."*

If the prospective employer is a known conservative and your profession (say a lawyer's) calls for a structured résumé, read Chapter 5, "Nuts and Bolts" right through. You will get hands-on training on standardized résumé writing. The chapter is self-contained. All the important information on form and content will be found right there.

If you have already written your résumé, but have time to revise, go through the self-assessment procedure in *Chapter 6, "Rate Your Résumé"*. You will pick up valuable pointers for improving your handiwork. Yes, chances are that you may have to rewrite a great deal and edit and polish quite a bit more. But, after putting in all that elbow grease, your efforts will sparkle like a rare gem. It will be a lot of work, but in the end, you will help only yourself!

If you have not yet written your résumé, read through the entire book. You will get a thorough understanding of the changes in philosophy and techniques that have revolutionized résumé writing the world over. We are confident that you will truly rediscover yourself, finding skills and capabilities that you could have overlooked in what you have written so far.

Chapter 8 "Bonus Section" is a special gift for you. It lists tried and tested job-hunting methods that enhance your success rate and accelerate your job search.

See *Chapter 9 "Sample Résumé"* for instances of résumé that illustrate the many principles explained in this book, including some overseas examples as well.

Conventions

Key points are highlighted throughout this book by using bold text in a box on the left side of the paragraph and some text matter have also been put in screen box to highlight it. See the sample titled "key thoughts in bold text" on the left side of this paragraph, which has been written in bold.

Key thoughts in bold text.

TIP

When important information exceeds a few lines and extends over an entire paragraph, a wise owl identifies it as a "TIP". You will find these tips distributed throughout, guiding you from one good idea to the next. Follow the owl and rapidly assimilate many good tips!

TRAP

All endeavours have dangers and pitfalls. Writing your résumé is no exception. It is easy to overlook errors or to overdo the publicity. You may give out wrong signals or to make untenable claims which are likely to be exposed later. A "TRAP" is clearly identified in this book by the familiar skull and crossbones. Beware when you see this symbol and save yourself grief!

Contents

1. Bag that Interview!

The Importance of Being Noticed

Imagine this scenario. You have applied for the job of your dreams. Your résumé has been painstakingly prepared. Spread over four pages, you have put down full details of your education and experience. You have dispatched your résumé and you wait for the interview call with bated breath!

At the receiving end, the personnel manager wades through 300 other résumés before wearily picking up your 4-page magnum opus. It is already 7 O'clock in the evening. What do you think will happen to your résumé? You guessed it! It will suffer a quick and unceremonious journey to the waste paper basket! Bad news!

But there is good news for you in this book! The good news is that you too can write an arresting, riveting

> **The good news is that you too can write arresting, riveting résumé.**

résumé that will stand out amongst the pile and will call attention to it. The skills are not difficult to learn after you have shed some of the old notions of what a résumé must be.

This book will guide you as you acquire that killing edge, that little extra, which almost guarantees an interview call. You will unlearn some old and outdated tricks, learn many new ones and most important, acquire the skills to identify the jobs that truly match your abilities. You will learn to market yourself attractively without deviating from the truth. Read on for an exhilarating and rewarding experience!

What is a Résumé?

Let us begin right at the beginning. A résumé has just one objective, to make sure that you get called for the interview!

You are trying to enroll the reader of your résumé, not to educate him. The interview will give you all the opportunity you need to convey information about your education, experience and special skills. The résumé is to make sure that you actually get this opportunity. A résumé is an advertisement of yourself, disguised as the story of your professional life. Like the trailer of a suspense movie, a résumé whets the appetite. A trailer is successful only if the audience come back to see the actual movie. A résumé is successful only if you get called to the interview. It is as simple as that.

A résumé is an advertisement of yourself, disguised as story of your professional life.

What a Résumé is Not

It is a mistake to think of your résumé as a history of your past, as a personal statement or as some sort of self-expression. No doubt, most of the content of the résumé is focused on your job history. But, you must train yourself to write with the intention of creating interest. Your aim is to persuade the employer to call you. If you write with that goal, your final product will be very different from just a catalogue of your education and the jobs you have held so far.

> **You must train yourself to write with the intention of creating interest.**

If you realize, that a great résumé can be your ticket to getting exactly the job you want, you will be able to muster genuine enthusiasm for creating a real masterpiece. This is your key to the creation of a masterpiece rather than the feeble product that most people turn out.

TRAP Most people write a résumé because they know that they have to write one to get a job. They write their résumé grudgingly, to fulfil this obligation. In the hierarchy of worldly delights, writing your résumé is considered only slightly more exciting than filling out your income tax form! That is the wrong approach!

The "Killer" Edge

Research has shown that depending on the level of the job applied for, only one interview is granted for every 300 to 500 résumés received by the average employer. Research also tells us that your résumé will be quickly scanned, rather than read. 10 to 20 seconds is all the time you have to persuade a prospective employer to read further. What this means is that the decision to interview a candidate is usually based on an overall first impression of the résumé. The quick screening must so impress the reader that it convinces him of the candidate's qualifications and an interview results.

10 to 20 seconds is all the time you have to persuade an employer to read further.

TIP

To write an effective résumé, you have to learn how to write powerful, but subtle advertising copy. Not only that, but you must sell a product in which you have large personal investment: you. Given the fact that most of us do not naturally think in a marketing-oriented way, this is not easy. Even more difficult is to shed your natural reticence and to sell anything, least of all, yourself. But, if you want to increase your job-hunting effectiveness as much as possible, you will have to learn how to write a spectacular résumé.

The top half of the first page of your résumé will either make you or break you. By the time he has read the first few lines, you have either caught the reader's interest, or your résumé has failed.

Remember that you do not need to use hard selling tactics. Certainly, you will not make any claim that is not absolutely true. However, you do need to get over your modesty and unwillingness to toot your own horn. In real life, it is important to remember that people often buy the best-advertised product rather than the best product!

> **Certainly, you will not make any claim that is not absolutely true.**

If you put in a little extra effort to create an excellent résumé, you will find that you will get a better response from prospective employers than people with better credentials. This is why it is worth your while to master the tools and the techniques that you will meet in this book. Give us your undivided attention and we promise to give you that "killer" edge in the job market.

The Bad News!

The bad news is that your present résumé is probably much more inadequate than you now realize. You will have to learn how to think and write in a style that will be completely new to you.

Pitfalls to Avoid

You should not include any negative information in your résumé. Remember that a résumé is a marketing document, which should focus on your strengths and achievements! Read through the section below to get a flavour of how you must adjust your style to avoid pitfalls in writing your résumé.

> **Do not include any negative information.**

Periods of Unemployment

What did you do while you were unemployed? If you took training courses, mention it in your résumé. Probably, you were self-employed or working part-time. If you have been unemployed for only a few months, use full years on your résumé.

Too Little Experience or Education

Probably, you have some vacation or unpaid job experience that supports the job that you seek. If your work experience is not related to the position you are applying for, focus on your educational achievements. Draft your résumé to present your strengths first.

Too Old

Avoid displaying dates. Instead of a detailed list of all the jobs held, focus on the ones that strengthen your candidature for the job you are applying for. Avoid a long chronological listing.

Too Young

Again, avoid displaying dates. Display information of your summer jobs or in-house training experience in the same format as your permanent job positions. Provide details of your responsibilities and achievements. Consider using a résumé format that will focus on your skills rather than displaying information chronologically.

Integrity

While pitfalls like these are to be avoided, please be very sure that the information you provide never deviates from the truth. You are allowed only to represent facts in a favourable light, but not to invent them. As in a game of cricket, you may apply a positive spin, but you may not "doctor" the ball!

Emergency!

Let us assume that you have to mail your résumé tomorrow. You have no time to go through this book before writing the urgently needed résumé. To cope with such an emergency, given below is a "bare-bones" outline for the last minute résumé-writer. It will not generate the best résumé, but it will probably get you off the hook this time! If it does not work, then read this book right through and begin again. Your next effort will be a great deal better.

A "bare-bones" outline for emergency use!

A Last Minute Guide Book

- Write what the employer wants to hear. Put yourself in his shoes and try to imagine what he is looking for in the ideal candidate for the job. Be truthful, however. You will have to backup your claims in the interview!
- Focus on those points in your education, skill or employment that support your candidature for the job you are applying for. You may have spent a short time doing a similar job and much longer time doing something else of a different nature. Make sure that the relevant job is displayed more prominently than the less relevant jobs.
- Focus on your strengths and achievements. Dwell on scholarships, awards or honourable mentions. Speak of problems solved, targets met, goals achieved.
- Prioritise the information. Give priority to achievements or events most relevant to the job, you are targeting. It may be better to dispense with the

chronological approach in order to bring to the forefront some past achievement without creating the feeling that nothing noteworthy has happened thereafter.

- Keep your résumé 1-2 pages long, unless your job is of highly scientific or technical in nature. As we have already seen, the first 15 to 20 seconds of reading will seal the fate of your résumé. The key messages must be conveyed in the top half of the first page of your résumé!
- Make it easy to read. Use bullets, white space and short sentences. Use active rather than passive voice.
- There must be absolutely no spelling or grammatical errors!
- Ask your friend to comment on your résumé. However, it is your résumé! Make the suggested changes only if you are one hundred percent certain that the suggestions will improve your résumé!

A Second Look at this Book!

If the suggestions given above help you to land your job, then congratulations! You need not read this book any further, for now. However, it is not the end of your career. Time will come again to put another résumé together. Before you do that, may we suggest that you read the rest of the book right through?

Words of Wisdom

If you are reading this section, it means that you have decided to read the whole book and not stop after going through the last minute guide book in the earlier section.

Before plunging deep into the art of résumé writing, we may wish to stop and recapitulate what we have discussed so far. Here is a summary.

Do Not be Modest

Many of us are hesitant to put down just how much we have done, or how good we are. We grow up being taught not to brag, but this is your chance! A résumé is like a sales prospectus, and you are the product. The résumé gets you the job interview, and then it's up to you to close the sale and land the job! Therefore, make sure you do not leave out any of the relevant good stuff from your résumé!

Select Statements with Impact

The statement: "Effectively managed a diverse population of 30 computer professionals to become a cohesive working team" is effective; "Am excellent with people and have great managerial skills" is not. "Consistently exceeded production quotas by 30 to 50 %" is effective; "Am very good at getting a lot of work done" is not.

Keep it Honest

You want to say as much as you can that's positive about yourself, but remember, if the résumé works, it will get you an interview with someone who will probably be looking right at it during that interview. Do not ever put in anything you cannot defend, justify or comfortably explain.

Presentation is Important

While the content of your résumé is a very important thing, the visual appearance can also make a big difference. If your résumé is packed with great information, but appears crowded and hard to read, a busy executive might just not take the time to go through it with the care it deserves. Unfair? Of course, but this is the real world! Use indentations, bulleted points, and lots of white space. Put two or three short or medium sized sentences with bullet points, although sometimes, one key statement with real impact should stand alone, by itself.

For readability, use indentations, bullets and lots of white space.

Writing an Effective Résumé

In the sections that follow, we will plunge right into the art of résumé writing in earnest. To give you a preview of what we will encounter, here are some more tips on writing an outstanding résumé. See also the tips in the previous section titled "Words of Wisdom" for a complete picture.

Use the Appropriate Amount of Space

If you've been in the work force for five years, and are applying for your second job, using a two-page résumé would not be helpful. No one wants to look through a lot of padding. On the other hand, if you've been working for twenty years and have lots of experience and several jobs, trying to compress it into one page will never do you justice. In that case, forget the so called "experts" who recommend only one page, and use the space you need to get the job done right (and get the job!). This is especially true if you have a difficult situation to contend with, such as changing careers, or a scattered work history. About half of all résumés ever written could be fitted on one page without losing any punch. Another half does require two pages to do the material justice. Top executive level jobs (we are speaking of CEO's here!) may even merit 3 or 4 pages.

TIP

If you do use more than one page, use the top half of your covering letter to convey the punch. The covering letter will do the attention getting and ensure that your résumé is read.

Functional Versus Chronological

If you're on a simple career path, and your last job provides the most relevant experience for the job being applied for, a standard chronological résumé is generally best. Here you list your employment from the last to the first, and insert details of your experience under each employer. However, if you are changing careers, going back to something you used to do, or have a scattered work history, then a functional résumé will probably serve your needs better. This kind lists your achievements first, dividing them into two, three or four categories. Append your employment history afterwards with relatively little comment. If your résumé is more than one page, as most functional résumés are, be sure that the information most relevant to the job are all fitted on the first page itself.

Avoid "Buzzword Mania"

Most fields have some professional "jargon", and it's important to include enough technical terms to let your future employer know that you're familiar with their industry. This can be especially important in high-tech fields like computers or engineering. To an extent, it is also true in

An effective résumé gives a sense of who you are and what your future employer can expect you to accomplish.

industries as diverse as insurance, construction, nursing, etc. However, avoid résumés that are little more than a collection of buzzwords, and while these may show familiarity with the industry, they do nothing at all to set you apart as an employee from anyone else in the field. An effective résumé gives some sense of who you are (at least as far as your professional life is concerned), and what your future employer can expect you to accomplish for him. Let's face it; your value to your future employer is the bottom line for him.

Make Sure of Your First Impression

As the old saying goes, *"you never get a second chance to make a first impression!"* If your prospective employer receives hundreds (or even thousands) of résumés, unless you can get his attention, he will never get to know you, even if you are the most qualified. Even if you do get the interview, if your résumé is mediocre, that interview will start with you fighting an uphill battle to counter a weak first impression. So, take the time to get your résumé right! In exceptional circumstances, seek assistance from a professional who can give you that extra edge. Many successful, talented, and creative people, who are excellent in their professions, still choose to get help for their résumé. They know that their talents lie in other directions, and want every possible advantage for their careers. That is one big reason why they're successful in the first place! However, do read this book thoroughly first, before calling in an expert.

You never get a second chance to make a first impression!

❑❑❑

2. Covering Letters

If you send a résumé, you will usually enclose it with a covering letter. However, having discussed so much about the absolute need to create a strong first impression concisely, a valid question that we must now deal with is whether we need a covering letter at all. If we do, then under what circumstances do we need a covering letter? What should go on the covering letter and what should remain on the résumé? We look first, at the question of whether a covering letter is really necessary.

Do You Need a Covering Letter?

Unless you are handing over your résumé to the employer directly during the interview, we strongly advise you to include a covering letter with your résumé.

> **We strongly advise you to include a covering letter with your résumé.**

If you have not had any previous contact with the employer, a covering letter is a must. If you are targeting a newspaper advertisement or contacting someone whom you have been advised to get in touch with by your friend, your aunt or whoever, you should definitely include a covering letter explaining how you happened to apply.

If you have arranged an interview with the potential employer over the telephone and are sending your résumé to him, you should also include a covering letter referring to the phone conversation.

Even if you are sending your résumé to an old friend of yours, you should attach a covering letter explaining why you are looking for a job and why you are the best person to hire.

Why do You Need It?

It takes time to go through a résumé. Employers decide from the covering letter whether the résumé is worth that time.

A covering letter is like the cover of a paperback book. The chances are that a potential customer will not even pick up and leaf through the book unless its cover attracts him. Your résumé is in a similar situation. Most employers only scan through the résumé and then read the covering letter, so your covering letter has to be as well prepared as your résumé. Unless you have a very strong "Objective" statement, your résumé does not say why you are looking for a new job and why you are interested in the position you are targeting. So, the covering letter has to answer these questions.

Most employers only scan through a résumé and then read the covering letter.

TIP

Many organizations insist on a standard printed out application form. Such a form will severely restrict your opportunity to highlight aspects of your education or experience that will help you to stand out amongst the hundreds. The covering letter gives you a chance to catch attention, structure what you have to say, demonstrate your writing skills and provide evidence that you have studied the company and the job.

The purpose of the customised covering letter is to communicate a personalised message to a specific employer, answering the most fundamental employment question: "Why should I hire you?" You answer that in your covering letter, and the likelihood of an interview is at least doubled thereby.

To Whom?

Never ever address the covering letter "To whom it may concern" or "Human Resource Department". Many executives are known to discard all applications addressed to a position title on the grounds that if the applicant is too lazy to find out his name, he will be too lazy to do a good job as well.

Never ever address a covering letter to "To whom it may concern"!

Send your résumé and covering letter to the person who can make the hiring decision. Most likely it will be the individual in charge of the department you would like to work in.

Do not aim too high. Presidents and members of management boards get lots of résumé because they are so visible. Find a person at the department or division level - ideally the person you would work for if you get the job.

TIP

Spend time to locate who is the person most likely to hire you and address the letter to him. Call the potential employer to find out. Do not worry if it takes three or more calls. If you get stuck, call the president's office to find who is in charge of the department you want to work for.

Do not say that you are looking for a job. Say that you have some information to send and that you want to make sure it gets to the right person.

Unless you know the person very well, use "Mr." or "Ms." in address, for example Dear Ms. Springs or Mr. Jones.

Be sure to spell the name correctly. It is amazing how many applications include miss-spelt names.

Structure

Your covering letter has to answer the following questions:

What Position are You Applying for?

State it clearly and at once. Better go straight to the point than beat about the bush.

How did You Learn about the Position or Company?

Did you learn about the opening through word-of-mouth or read about it in a newspaper advertisement? Just one sentence will answer the first two questions, such as "I am interested in a position of sales director in white goods division which you recently advertised in "The Times of India".

Why are You Applying for this Position?

Say some good words about the company you are targeting, which you can later use as a platform for presenting your own strengths, such as "HLL is well known for its innovative approach in product distribution, in particular, through web-based sales channels." Later, your strength as a web designer will fit in well with this opening statement.

Why are You the Best Person for the Position?

Choose 3 or 4 main points proving that you are the most suited candidate. Focus on your strengths and achievements in the previous jobs. For example "I have 6 years experience in retail distribution of consumer products, including white goods. During my 3-year employment with Best Consumer Products Manufacturer, its white goods sales increased threefold. I have also been heavily involved in establishing one of the first retail distribution channels on the Internet for All India Manufacturers. As the position matches my qualifications and experience, I can be a productive director from 'day one'. The enclosed résumé outlines my skills and experience in more detail." As you can see, the candidate is relating the company's strengths – innovative sales approach with his own strength – involvement in web-based distribution channels.

Choose two or three main points proving that you are the best candidate.

What happens next? Try to take initiative in your hands. Do not just write "I hope to hear from you soon". Better "I will call you next week to see if we might schedule a convenient time to meet and discuss employment with your company."

More Tips on Covering Letters

Be Brief

To answer the questions we just discussed, the covering letter should not be longer than 3 to 4 paragraphs. 1 to 2 paragraphs should be enough to answer the first three questions. You should not spend more than 1 to 2 paragraphs on the fourth question.

Make the Reader Interested

Communicate something personal. In your opening lines write something that is associated with the person, company or division you are applying to. The likelihood of personal response to your letter is directly proportional to the degree of personal attention you put in your covering letter.

Here is an opening that goes straight to the point:

"Dear Mr. Shah,

Our mutual friend Mrs. Venugopal urged me to write you about your plan to setup a research department. I would like to help you to set it up - and I know how to do it, as you can see from my résumé".

Sell Yourself

Just like a résumé, your covering letter is a marketing document. Do not try to tell the story of your life! Instead, tell the employer what he wants to hear. For example, "My engineering experience with M/s Bridge Construction Company would be valuable to you in your new construction project."

Be Specific and Factual

Offer evidence in support of your strengths and achievements. Touch on your most important achievements in a matter-of-fact style.

Use Their Language

Use the right terms to indicate your skills and qualifications. Watch out however for overuse of jargon.

You must have noticed by now that the general rules for covering letters are very similar to the ones you have seen so far for the résumé themselves. No wonder, since both of them have only one purpose, to get you that interview!

This concludes our preliminary overview of résumé and covering letters. We will now get our hands dirty and get down to actual résumé writing in the next two chapters beginning with the all-important step called "Preparation".

❑❑❑

3. Preparation

Brainstorm

Focus on your writing skills. Understand clearly what the employer is looking for and what you have to offer before you begin writing your résumé. Write your answers to the question, "What would make someone the perfect candidate for this job?" Write on notebook paper, one answer per page. Arrange the sheets of paper in the order of importance of the qualities or abilities that you think would be most important to the interviewer. Then, starting with the top priority page, fill the rest of that page (or as much of it as you can), about why you are the person who best fulfils the employer's needs. Write down everything you have ever done that demonstrates that you fit perfectly with what is wanted and needed by the prospective employer. Later, you

> **Write your answer to the question "What would make someone the perfect candidate for this job?"**

will edit what you have written to eliminate what is not relevant.

What is Your USP?

The whole idea is to loosen up your thinking enough so that you can see some new connections between what you have done and what the employer is looking for. You need not confine yourself to work-related accomplishments. Use your entire life as the palette to paint with. If the football club or your former gang is the only place where you have demonstrated your special gift for teaching and leadership, fine, use those examples! The point is to cover all possible ways of thinking about and communicating what do you do well. What are the talents you bring to the market place? What do you have to offer the prospective employer? If you are making a career change or a young person new to the job market, you have to be especially creative in getting across the qualities that make you outstanding. These brainstorming pages will be the raw material from which you can craft your résumé.

These brainstorming pages will be the raw material from which you craft your résumé.

One important part of the planning process is to decide which résumé format fits your needs best. Don't automatically assume that a traditional format will work best for you.

What does the Employer Really Want?

Undoubtedly, jobs vary and so do the qualities that best suit the job requirements. Still, we observe that some people have a very successful professional life. The sun always shines upon their careers. No matter how many job changes they make, they succeed, spectacularly. Clearly, they possess some key qualities that bring them success in every job they take. What are these qualities that every employer wants?

What are the key qualities that every employer wants?

Employers agree that the candidates who have excellent communication skills, good grooming habits and relevant work experience impress them. Employers also say that they want trustworthy employees who can move right in, get along with their co-workers, and get the job done without having to be guided at each step. Let us look closely at what employers want.

The Top Ten Qualities Employers Seek

- Communication skills (verbal and written)
- Honesty/integrity
- Teamwork skills (working well with others)
- Interpersonal skills (relating well to others)
- Motivation/initiative
- Strong work ethics
- Analytical skills
- Flexibility/adaptability
- Computer skills
- Self-confidence

These qualities (not shown here in any particular order) are appreciated in all employees, whether you have years of experience or are new to the job market.

New Hire Skills

These are the top seven skills (not in any particular order) that employers look for in persons new to the job market, perhaps on their first or second jobs.

- Interpersonal
- Teamwork
- Leadership
- Analytical
- Verbal communication
- Written communication
- Computer

No matter what the job level or what type of organization; your value to the employer will be enhanced if your résumé and covering letter focuses on at-least some of these qualities. Your past track record should demonstrate that you have exhibited some of these qualities during your professional career.

When writing up your résumé, go back to the notes that you had prepared while brainstorming (see earlier in this chapter) and let your performance record reflect how some of these desirable qualities came to the fore. Do so with flair and your résumé will become irresistible to any employer!

Having created an outline of the contents by brainstorming as we have seen above, we need to now focus on the presentation of the contents by analysing the structure of outstanding résumé. We do so in the next chapter.

❑❑❑

4. Structure

Two Styles of Résumé

In this book, we have placed a great deal of emphasis on the "Advertisement" style for both résumé and covering letters. However, there are situations where the résumé is expected to follow a well-established format, conveying information rather than scoring selling points. The formal style cannot be ignored in many professions such as law, medicine and accounting. For such job applications, you will have to conform to established practices. No doubt, a well-crafted covering letter provides subtle advertisement for you, but you have to format the résumé in the established "black tie and waistcoat" style, in order that it is considered at all.

"Advertisement" and "Formal" styles for résumé.

In this chapter, we will cover the "Advertisement" (or "Ad") style. In the next chapter, Chapter 5, "Nuts and Bolts", we will cover the more formal styles. Regardless of the style of the final writing however, we encourage you to think about your strengths and their relevance to the job, unconventionally. It will enrich your résumé and covering letter and increase your chances of an interview call even if your résumé is finally written in a "regulation" format.

Think unconventionally regardless of the final format.

A Great Résumé has Two Sections

In the first section, you make assertions about your abilities, qualities and achievements. You write powerful, but honest, advertising copy that makes the reader immediately perk up and realize that you are someone special. The second section, the evidence section, is where you back up your assertions with evidence that you actually did what you said, you did. This is where you list and describe the jobs you have held, your education, etc. This is all the mandatory stuff, you are obliged to include.

Unfortunately, most résumé have just the evidence section, with no assertions. If you have trouble going to sleep, just read a few résumé each night just before going to bed. You will fall asleep in no time! Unfortunately, the average résumé has the same soporific effect on the potential employer. But, that is not what you want. Rather, you want him to immediately reach for the phone and invite you for an interview when he has finished reading your résumé.

You want the potential employer to reach for the phone and call you for an interview when he finishes reading your résumé!

The résumé you have written in the past have probably been a gallant effort to inform the reader. You don't want them informed. You want them interested and excited. This is where the assertion section comes in. The juice is here!

You can judiciously distribute the assertions between the covering letter and the résumé itself. It is a good idea to first write the résumé and then pick up the key highlights from the assertion and the evidence sections to incorporate them in the covering letter.

The Assertion Section

There are two or three sub-sections in the assertion section. You begin the assertion section by stating your objective in applying for the job. This is followed by a summary of your most important qualifications, qualities and achievements. In exceptional cases, especially for high level appointments and for major career change situations, you may need a third sub-section that outlines your skills and accomplishments.

The Objective

Ideally, your résumé should subtly convey why you are the perfect candidate for the job Remember that good advertising is directed towards a very specific target audience. When a car company tries to sell their inexpensive compact to an older audience, they show grandfather and grandmother stuffing the car with many happy, contented and shiny grandchildren and talk about how safe and

Tailor your résumé to the prospective employer's needs.

economical the car is. When they advertise the very same car to the young executives, they show the car going around corners on two wheels, with plenty of drums and trumpets thundering in the background. You must be equally specific in focusing your résumé.

Targeting your résumé requires that you be absolutely clear about your career. The way to demonstrate your clarity of direction is to display the first major topic of your résumé as your objective.

Let us look at a real world example. Suppose the owner of a small software company puts an advertisement in the paper seeking an experienced software sales person. A week later the employer receives 3,000 résumé. The applicants have a bewildering variety of backgrounds. The employer has no way of knowing whether any of them are really interested in selling software. He knows that many of the résumé received are from people who are just using a shotgun approach, casting their seed to the winds. Then, he comes across a résumé in the pile that starts with the following:

OBJECTIVE

To seek a software sales position in an organization where an extraordinary record of generating new accounts, exceeding sales targets and enthusiastic customer relations, would be needed.

This wakes him up. He is immediately interested. This first sentence conveys some very important and powerful messages: "I want exactly the job you are offering. I am a superior candidate because I have the qualities that are most important to you. I want to make a contribution to your company." The message works well because the employer is smart enough to know that someone who wants to do exactly what he is offering will be much more likely to succeed than someone who doesn't. And, he will probably be a lot more pleasant to work with as well. The candidate has done a good job of establishing why he is the perfect candidate in his first sentence. He has thought about what qualities would make a candidate stand out. He has started communicating that he is capable of making a contribution to the employer. He is not writing from a self-centred point of view.

Use the objective to establish why you are the perfect candidate for the job.

Even when people are smart enough to provide an objective, they often make the mistake of saying something like, "a position where I can hone my skill as a scissors sharpener." or something similar. The employer is interested in hiring you for what you can do for him, not for fulfilling your private goals and agenda.

How to Write an Objective

Here's how to write your objective. First of all, decide on a specific job title for your objective. Then go back to your list of answers to the question "How can I demonstrate that I am the perfect candidate?" What are the two or three qualities, abilities or achievements that would make a candidate stand out as truly exceptional for that specific job? The applicant in the above example recognized that

Be sure that the objective is to the point. Do not use fluffy phrases.

the prospective employer has a small, growing Software Company. Therefore, he would be very interested in a candidate with an ability to generate new accounts. So, he made that the very first point in his résumé. Be sure the objective is to the point. Do not use fluffy phrases, which are obvious, or do not mean anything, such as: "allowing the ability to enhance potential and utilize my experience in new challenges." An objective may be broad and still somewhat undefined in some cases, such as: "a mid-level management position in the hospitality or entertainment industry." Remember, your résumé will only get a few seconds attention, at best! You have to generate interest right away, in the first sentence they lay their eyes on. Having an objective statement that really sizzles is highly effective. And it's simple to do. One format is:

OBJECTIVE: An Xxx position in an organization where Yyy and Zzz would be needed.

Xxx is the name of the position you seek. Yyy and Zzz are the most compelling qualities, abilities or achievements that will really make you stand out above the crowd of applicants. The research you have previously done to find out what is most important to the employer will provide the information to fill in Yyy and Zzz.

Be prepared to write separate and specific résumé, written in appropriate style, for each job that you apply for. There is nothing wrong with having several different résumé, each with a different objective, each specifically crafted for a different type of position.

A résumé is a subtle advertisement copy, not the story of your life!

You may even want to change some parts of your résumé for each job you apply for. Remember to create an objective that is perfectly matched with the job. Remember also that you are writing advertising copy, not the story of your life!

TIP

The point of using an "Objective" is to create a very specific psychological response in the mind of the reader. If you are making a career change or you are a young person, you want the employer to immediately focus on where you are going, rather than where you have been. If you are looking for another job in your present field, it is more important to stress your qualities, achievements and abilities, first.

A few examples of separate "objective" sections now follow:

- Senior staff position with a bank that offers the opportunity to utilize my expertise in commercial real estate loans and strategic management.
- An entry-level position in the hospitality industry where a background in advertising and public relations would be needed.
- A position in teaching English as a second language where a special ability to motivate and communicate effectively with students would be needed.

The Summary

The "summary" or "summary of qualifications" consists of several concise statements that focus the reader's attention on the most important qualities, achievements and abilities you have to offer. Those qualities should be the most compelling demonstrations of why they should hire you instead of the other candidates. It gives you a brief opportunity to telegraph a few of your most sterling qualities. It is your one and only chance to attract and hold their attention, to get across what is most important, and to entice the employer to keep reading.

The summary may be the only section fully read by the employer!

This is the spiciest part of the résumé. This may be the only section fully read by the employer, so it should be very strong and convincing. The summary is the one place to include professional characteristics (extremely energetic, a gift for solving complex problems in a fast-paced environment, a natural salesman, exceptional interpersonal skills, committed to excellence, etc.), which may be helpful in winning the interview. Direct every word in the summary to your targeted goal.

How to Write a Summary

How to write a "Summary"? Go back to your lists that answer the question, "What would make someone the ideal candidate?" Look for the qualities the employer will care about most. Then look at what you wrote about why you are the perfect person to fill their need. Pick the stuff that best demonstrates why they should hire you. Assemble it into your summary section. The most common ingredients of a well-written summary are as follows. Use the ones that highlight you best.

- A short phrase describing your profession,

- Followed by a statement of broad or specialized expertise;
- Followed by two or three additional statements related to any of the following:
  - Breadth or depth of skills.
  - Unique mix of skills.
  - Range of environments in which you have experience.
  - A special or well-documented accomplishment.
  - A history of awards, promotions, or superior performance commendations.
  - One or more professional or appropriate personal characteristics.
  - A sentence describing your professional objective or interest.

If You are Making a Career Change

Notice that the examples below show how to include your objective in the "summary" section. If you are making a career change, the summary section must show how well your past experience has prepared you to do what you seek to do in the future.

> **The summary should show how well your past experience prepares you for the job applied for.**

If you are a young person new to the job market, your "summary" will be based more on ability than on experience.

Examples of "Summary" Sections

- Highly motivated, creative and versatile real estate executive with seven years of experience in property acquisition, development and construction, as well as the management of large apartment complexes. Especially skilled at building effective, productive working relationships with clients and staff. Excellent management, negotiation and public relations skills. Seeks a challenging management position in the real estate field that offers extensive contact with the public.

- Over 10 years as an organizational catalyst/training design consultant with a track record of producing extraordinary results for more than 20 national and non-government organizations. A commitment to human development and community service. Energetic self-starter with excellent analytical, organizational, and creative skills.
- Financial Management Executive with nearly ten years of experience in banking and international trade, finance, investments and economic policy. Innovative in structuring credit enhancement for corporate as well as personal financing. Skilled negotiator with strong management, sales and marketing background. Areas of expertise include: (a bulleted list of areas of expertise should follow this paragraph.)
- Health Care Professional experienced in management, program development and policy making in India as well as in neighbouring countries. Expertise in emergency medical services. A talent for analysing problems, developing and simplifying procedures, and finding innovative solutions. Proven ability to motivate and work effectively with persons from other cultures and all walks of life. Skilled in working within a foreign environment and with limited resources.

Skills and Accomplishments

Assume that you are a top- or mid-level executive, wanting a significant career change or upward move. You want your professional career to blast off! You are going to need more details in your assertion section since you need to be more persuasive that you are truly outstanding and that you have the preparation, the talent and the will to make a big career change, or upward move, and succeed!

You are still writing to enroll the reader, not to inform him. Basically, you do exactly what you did in the previous section, except that you go into more details. In the summary, you focused on your most special highlights. Now you have to tell the "rest of the best" of your story! Let them know what results you produced, what happened as a result of your efforts, what you are especially gifted or experienced at doing. Flesh out the most important highlights in your summary.

You are writing to enrol the reader, not to inform him!

TIP

You are still writing to do what every good advertisement has to do well, communicating the following: "if you buy this product, you will get these direct benefits". If it does not contribute to furthering this communication, do not bother to say it. Remember, not too much detail. Preserve a bit of mystery. Don't tell them everything.

Sometimes the "Skills and Accomplishments" section is a separate section. In a chronological résumé, it becomes the first few phrases of the descriptions of the various jobs you have held. When it is a separate section, it can have several possible titles, depending on your situation, such as:

- Skills and accomplishments.
- Selected accomplishments.
- Recent accomplishments.
- Areas of expertise.
- Career highlights.
- Professional highlights.

The Structure

There are a number of different ways to structure "Skills and Accomplishments" sections. In all of these styles, put your skills and accomplishments in order of importance for the desired career goal. If you have many skills, the last skill paragraph might be called "Additional Skills".

Here are a few ways you could structure your "Skills and Accomplishments" section:

1. A listing of selected skills or accomplishments or a combination of both, with bullets:

    - Raised Rs. 10 Lakh in 21 days in flood relief collection drive.
    - Conducted legal research for environmental group on the use of CFL gas.
    - Coordinated the annual company wide goal setting meeting.

2. A list of bulleted accomplishments or skill paragraphs under each job (in a chronological résumé).

General Manger of Sales and Marketing at Export Sales Corporation, Mumbai.

- Promoted from Sales Representative within two years of joining company to GM of Sales and Marketing. Responsible for international sales of raw materials, as well as printing and graphic arts equipments. Oversaw five sales managers. Was in charge of direct sales and marketing in 7 countries throughout the Middle East.
- Recruited, trained and managed sales staff. Developed marketing strategy, prepared sales projections and established quotas. Selected and contracted with overseas sub-agents to achieve international market penetration.
- Negotiated and finalized long-term contractual agreements with suppliers on behalf of clients. Oversaw all aspects of transactions, including letters of credit, international financing, preparation of import/export documentation, and shipping/freight forwarding.
- Planned and administered sales and marketing budget, and maintained sole profit/loss responsibility. Within first year, doubled company's revenues, and produced Rs. 300 Crore in annual sales during the next three years.

The Evidence Section

No résumé has a formal "Evidence" section, with such a title! However, whatever you assert, must be supported by evidence and this evidence is attached in the conventional format with headings such as:

There is no formal "evidence" section!

- Education.
- Experience.
- Awards won or papers published.
- Membership of professional bodies.

Compelling evidence is absolutely necessary. No résumé can only make assertions and not back up the claims! In the next section, we shall go into the details of how to present evidence in your résumé.

Three Kinds of Résumé

There are two basic kinds of résumé. The third kind is really a combination of the first two:

- Chronological résumé.
- Skills or Functional résumé.
- Combination résumé.

TIP

Which one is best for you depends on many factors such as your experience level, the level of the job being applied for, the employer and the sector of the industry, whether you are applying for a promotion or a career change and so on.

Here are some guidelines to help you decide what is best for the job you are applying for.

Chronological résumé present your life experience in a chronological format. They focus on what have you been doing and what you have achieved. They provide a clear picture of your employment history, focusing on career advancement and increased responsibilities. If your previous education and work experience support the job you are applying for, you may use a chronological résumé. A big advantage of a chronological résumé is that it is easy to do. A simple chronological résumé can be completed in 3 or 4 hours!

Skills Résumé, sometimes called **Functional Résumé**, focus on the skills you have acquired while working. It clusters the skills/knowledge you have gained under major skills areas. A skills résumé is a better alternative if you are changing careers and do not have much of relevant work experience in the job you are applying for.

TRAP Employers sometimes dislike the skills résumé, as it does not provide a clear picture of your employment history. Skills résumé does not answer the questions many employers are asking themselves when they first look at your résumé such as "How well has the applicant performed in his job? Has he been promoted? Has he been given increased responsibilities?"

At the same time, most employers will admit that a list of your core skills and abilities definitely adds value to your résumé. It allows you to demonstrate your strengths in relation to the position you are targeting.

TIP

Therefore, we advise you to use a combination résumé in most cases. It includes the better of the two generic résumé types. First, outline the skills and knowledge relevant for the position you are applying for. Then continue with your work experience and educational background supporting the skills you have with specific examples.

We shall now look at all the three types of résumé in detail.

Chronological Résumé

A chronological résumé presents your professional experience in a chronological format. Chronological résumé focuses on what you have been doing and what you have achieved. Chronological résumé work best if your previous job experience and education supports the position you are applying for.

Many employers prefer chronological résumé to skills résumé as it provides a clear picture of your employment history, focusing on career advancement and increased responsibilities.

What to Include in a Chronological Résumé

- Name and contact details.

Include your full name and contact details: address, phone numbers and email. If you are planning to move, include the new address and the date from which you will be accessible at the new location.

- Job objective.

If you are targeting a specific job opening (e.g. marketing assistant in a large service organization), you can use the title of the position you are applying for. Otherwise, avoid using narrow job titles.

> **TRAP** Do not try to target a whole universe of positions. The employers would not like to employ someone who does not seem to know what he wants. Do not include meaningless job objectives such as "a challenging and well paid position in a creative environment".

Selecting a job objective may be a time consuming process, but it will certainly pay off. Based on the job objective, you will be able to decide on the experiences/training most relevant to the position, you are targeting.

- Work experience.

Start with the most recent position.

Indicate the organization you worked for, your job title, employment dates, major responsibilities and achievements.

Focus and provide more details about the jobs that support your job objective.

If you worked for a small, not so well-known organization, indicate the type of business it is engaged in. Provide details of the city, state or province in which the organization is located.

TIP

As your job title, include one that describes your duties and responsibilities best, which may not necessarily be your formal title. For example, you might write "responsible for public relations", and not "assistant to vice-president", if that is what you did.

Include both your responsibilities and achievements. Do not simply write "Purchase Manager". Instead, use a more descriptive paragraph that will immediately follow the job title, as shown below:

> **Include both your responsibilities and achievements in your job title.**

"**Purchase Manager**. Through implementation of strict raw material inspection procedures and skilful negotiations with key suppliers achieved 10 per cent reduction in per unit raw material costs maintaining the same quality level".

The description of achievement adds punch to the job title.

- Education and training.

If you have a long employment history, focus on the relevant educational and training experiences.

TIP

Consider dropping the whole section, if your education and training do not support the job objective or if you do not have the education and credentials that are typically required for the type of position you are targeting.

If you are a recent graduate, your education is likely to be your most significant achievement! If you have good marks, put them down on your résumé. Focus on the subjects that directly support your job objective.

- Language skills, computer skills and other skills.

Be sure to mention multiple language fluency, skills with computers and any other skills relevant for the position you are applying for.

- Personal information.

Do not include any personal information, unless it strongly supports your job objective. For example, if you are applying for a position of an actor, you could include your height, weight, hair and eye colour. Otherwise, leave them out!

- References

You can include the names and contact details of 2 to 3 referees. Make sure that your referees give positive references by asking them how they would characterize you and your work. Include only those referees whose opinions of you and your work would be most beneficial. Another option is to prepare a separate list with the names of referees or, even better, get 2 to 3 of your referees to write letters of reference but provide them only upon request.

Letters of references are provided only upon request.

A Skills or Combination Résumé?

If you are changing career and have little or no experience related to the position you are applying for, you should use a skills résumé. Skills résumé focuses on the skills you have rather than work experience or education.

As we have already seen, employers sometimes dislike a skills résumé, as it does not provide them with a clear picture of your employment history.

Therefore, we advise you to select a combination résumé whenever possible, since it will present your skills and abilities, your relevant work experience and education in the best possible light.

Wherever possible, use a combination résumé.

What to Include in a Skills Résumé

- Name and contact details.
- Job objective.
- Skills, abilities and areas of expertise.

As its name suggests, skills résumé focuses on your core skills. Therefore, the major part of a skills résumé should be devoted to skills, abilities and areas of expertise.

Focus on skills, abilities and areas of expertise.

Identify the skills that are required for the position you are targeting. Compare the skills you believe are important for the position you are targeting and the skills you have.

Cluster the skills you have and those that are required for the position, grouping them under 4 to 6 sub-headings. Where ever possible, support your statements with facts. Do not write "good management skills" but support them with evidence. Write instead "managed a group of 8 people from different backgrounds." You can use sub-headings such as:

Where possible, support your statement with facts.

- Work experience.
- Education and training.
- Language skills, computer skills and other skill.s
- Personal information.
- References.

For details to be provided under each of the sub-headings see the previous section under "chronological résumé".

Suit Your Profile to the Job

We have discussed a large number of principles for writing an arresting résumé and covering letter. The central theme that emerges is that you must match your skills, aptitudes and abilities to the needs of the job, tailoring each résumé to specifically suit the needs of the job advertised.

In your desire to match job needs with your education, skills, and experience, do avoid the temptation to be too creative. It is important to realize that the résumé is only a first step. After getting an interview call, it will still be necessary to back-up your claims in the face-to-face interview.

TRAP

It goes without saying that not every job will match your own profile. While some change in emphasis may align your résumé closer to the job advertised, some will be obvious mismatches and are best left alone.

You will do better to target a job, which is more in line with your education and skill profile. Do not court disappointment by trying to fit a round profile in a square job!

Improve that Fit!

Assuming that there is a preliminary fit between what the employer wants and what you have to offer, here are suggestions for improving the thrust of your résumé and enhancing the fit between you and the job.

Build on Your Strengths

Identify your skills and qualifications. Ask yourself the following questions. Some hints are given to help you to reply.

1. What skills do you have?

   [Hint: Are you quick in making decisions? Or, do you have good negotiation skills?]

2. Which of the skills that you have will be useful for the job you are applying for?

   [Hint: Which of the key skills you listed above, you enjoy doing most? Try to prioritise them. Also, do you have any training specific to the job you are applying for?]

First, make a list of the key skills you possess. To help you, we have given a list of some key skills.

List of Skills

Loyal	Willin'g to Learn	Reliable	Hard Working
Creative	Responsible	Confident	Trustworthy
Ambitious	Energetic	Friendly	Flexible
Mature	Reliable	Communicative	Independent
Honest	Resourceful	Competent	Analytical
Negotiation	Budgeting	Supervision	Planning
Public Speaking	People Skills	Management Skills	Technical Skills

This is not an all-inclusive list, and should only serve as a guide in developing your own list of your skills. Do take your time in preparing this list. It may be the most important step in planning your career!

Next, relate your skills to the needs of the job. For example, if you are applying for the job of an office assistant, your knowledge of word-processing software will be a good selling point. Or, if you are applying for an overseas job, then, having a passport will be a big plus point.

Take a proactive stance. If you believe that you need additional training to be able to perform the job you want, take a suitable course! Even if you have only enrolled in a relevant training programme before the job interview, you will have a powerful selling point in your favour when you are face to face with your prospective employer.

TIP

The employer is more likely to employ someone who shows that he is genuinely interested in the job by investing time and resources in obtaining the required skills on his own time.

Take the Employer's Style into Account

We have touched upon the importance of taking into account the employer's own style of functioning while deciding between the modern "advertisement" style of résumé and the more conservative styles such as the "chronological" style.

Therefore, before writing, some research about the employer is necessary. These days, many companies have websites and you can gain valuable information about the company's size, performance and product range by visiting their web site. The local chamber of commerce will generally have old copies of the company's annual reports, which is another source of useful information about the company.

Some research about the employer is necessary.

TIP

Ultra conservative organizations wanting to hire professionals such as doctors or lawyers will favour a conventional résumé with only a muted and subtle sales pitch. The IT industry or the rapidly growing FMCG sales organizations on the other hand, will look for an aggressively structured résumé that promises action from the day you join them! Your style must match the employer's style!

Much of the information you collect will help you to select and highlight your relevant attributes, which will project you as the best candidate for the job. In addition, you will gain a feel of the organization from the website itself. Do they appear conservative or state of the art? You can adjust your "sales pitch" accordingly.

Put Yourself in the Employer's Place

Imagine that you are the person who will do the hiring. Do not think of some anonymous paper pusher deep in the bowels of the personnel department. Usually, the person who makes the hiring decision is also the person who is responsible for the bottom line productivity of the project or group you hope to be a part of. This is a person who cares deeply how well the job will be done. You need to write your résumé to appeal directly to him.

Ask yourself: What would make someone the perfect candidate? If you are seeking a job in a field you know well, you probably already know what would make someone a superior candidate. If you are not sure, gather hints from the help wanted advertisement you are answering, ask people who work in the same company or the same field. You could even call the prospective employer and ask them what they want. Do not make wild guesses in your résumé. It is very important to do this step well. If you are not addressing the employer's real needs, he will not respond to your résumé.

Ask yourself, what would make someone the perfect candidate for the job advertised?

TIP

Putting yourself in the shoes of the person doing the hiring is the first and most important step in writing a résumé that markets you rather than describes your history. Every step in producing a finished document should be part of your overall intention to convey to the prospective employer that you are a truly exceptional candidate in their eyes!

❑❑❑

5. Nuts and Bolts

Not all résumé require a very high level of creativity or startling originality of approach in either their content or form. There are conservative organizations looking for entry-level candidates. If your target job falls in this category, you may wish to adopt a fairly well established procedure without excessive frills. This chapter is a straightforward guide for writing regular résumé. Follow the guidelines given here and you will turn out perfectly serviceable résumé in a short time.

This chapter is a straightforward guide for writing regular résumé.

To get a serviceable résumé prepared quickly, some readers may use Chapter 5 straightaway without reading the first 4 chapters. For their benefit, the gists of the previous chapters have been covered here. If you are reading the book right through, these will provide a good way to revise what you have learnt already.

TIP

By combining some of the "selling" and "focusing" techniques discussed in the first 4 chapters with the "hands-on" approach of this chapter, entry level candidates can crank up the quality of their résumé by several notches while mid to high-level candidate can put together a masterpiece.

Résumé Basics

Why do You Need a Résumé?

The main reason you should have a résumé is simple - most employers request one. And even if the employer does not ask for a résumé, it is easily the most efficient way to present your qualifications, skills and experience.

In addition, the résumé writing process itself will help you to crystallize your job objective and determine your major skills and achievements. Research shows that people who write better, more carefully thought-through résumé also perform very much better at the subsequent job interviews!

Which Résumé is Best for You?

There are two basic types of résumé:

- Chronological résumé, usually put in the reverse order, the last job first.
- Skills résumé.

Chronological résumé present your working life experience in a chronological format. A chronological résumé focuses on what you have been doing and what you have achieved.

This type of résumé provides a clear picture of your employment history, focusing on career advancement and gradually increasing job responsibilities.

The Skills résumé on the other hand, focuses on the skills you have acquired while working. It clusters the skills or knowledge you have gained under major skills areas. If you have strong job specific abilities, the skills résumé will showcase it to your advantage.

TIP

Select the format that shows your abilities to greater advantage for the job at hand. You may have to write your résumé using both styles. Then read them both objectively. Decide which of the two makes the most of your assets and creates a greater impact. That one is the style for you!

Make Your Résumé Interesting

Most résumé are boring. View your résumé as a marketing document, an effective way to communicate your strengths and achievements. Remember – the employer does not want to hear your life story. He is looking for the best person to do the job. Therefore, convince him that in you, he will find the man he seeks. Focus on your achievements. List the facts that support your achievements. Make the reader want to know more!

Appearance and Formatting

Here are a few simple rules. We shall assume that you are using some good word processing software to prepare the final draft of your résumé.

- Do not use fancy font styles! Arial and Times New Roman with font size between 10 and 12 are the most appropriate.
- Use bullets. Bullets help to structure your résumé. Bullets will also considerably improve the appearance and reading ease.
- Use white space. A crowded résumé "hides" the things you want to say.

TIP

You may have a conflict between a one-page target and an uncluttered appearance. If so, then appearance should score over the one page limitation. However, first make sure that all that you have included are vital to sell your candidature. Should you conclude that the case justifies two pages, go ahead. However, include the vital points of your job-worthiness in the first paragraph of your covering letter and use a powerful "Objective" statement on the first page of the résumé.

Length

- Unless you work in a highly scientific or technical field (4 and even more pages are regarded as a norm here), we suggest you keep your résumé 1 to 2 pages long.
- If you must exceed 1 page, then present key points in the top half of the first page.
- Present the key points. The résumé is a marketing document, which should only present the things that will be to your benefit.

- Use short sentences.
- Drop the "I", say "Achieved 10 per cent increase in sales" rather than "I achieved 10 per cent increase in sales."

How do I Write it?

Here is a step-by-step approach. When you complete the sections below, you will have the first draft of your résumé. It will be only a rough draft however and will require both formatting and editing.

When you have worked through the steps below, you will have the raw materials and know-how to construct your résumé. Then, you will need to decide on the type of résumé you wish to use (see "Which Résumé is Best for You?" earlier in this chapter), and then edit and polish it until it is in its final form. You will probably find the polishing to be the hardest part of writing your résumé.

You will probably find the polishing to be the hardest part.

So, let us get to the guts of a résumé. You may read the sections below either in sequence, or jump to the one you wish to learn more about. In each section, you will be introduced to the purpose, shown examples of how the section should look, and will be offered hints on how to get the job done. The sections are:

- Identifying Information.
- The Objective.
- Summary of Qualifications.
- Education.

- Work Experience.
- Activities/Interests.

Identifying Information

The first section of a résumé is your name, address, phone number, fax and e-mail address. You need not actually write the words "résumé" at the top, since it will be obvious to your reader what he is looking at. It is customary to put name, residential address and phone number(s) in this section. It may also be helpful to put your office phone number(s) and perhaps, fax and e-mail as well (but only if it is not a problem that you be contacted at your present job).

Most correspondence today comes via regular mail or phone but you never know what the future holds! So, add an e-mail address if you have one.

Examples

Here are just a couple of ways that you can display your identifying information. Remember, the goal is to quickly and effectively communicate who you are and how you can be contacted.

- Example #1

Jayant Neogy

E 2301 Palam Vihar,
Gurgaon, Haryana–122017
Email: Jlneogy@vsnl.com
Phone: 0124 636 9999

- Example #2

Jayant Neogy
E 2301 Palam Vihar,
Gurgaon, Haryana–122017
Email: jlneogy@vsnl.com
Phone: 0124 636 9999

Here is a simple format that should meet most résumé needs. Note the serial numbers for some tips about the form.

First Name	
Last Name	
Address, Street	
Address, City, State, Pin Code	
Residential Phone (1)	
Office Phone (2)	
Fax (3)	
E-Mail (4)	

Tips

1. Someone must be available at home during office hours.
2. Is it Okay to receive interview calls at your current office?
3. If available.
4. Do you check your e-mail regularly?

The Objective

The objective is an optional part of the résumé.

Is an Objective for You?

Here are some things to consider:

> **An objective defines the purpose of your application.**

If you know exactly what kind of work you wish to be considered for, then you might want to communicate that in your objective. Defining your purpose for your application is a very good way to start, especially if your application is not in response to an advertised vacancy and therefore, the reader does not know what type of job you have in mind.

When used, an objective serves the important purpose of telling an employer what position you are seeking. It should convey a sense of clarity in your mind regarding your very next step on your career path. The objective, therefore, should be focused and clearly stated. It should not be a general statement about your life goals.

The importance of a clear objective statement cannot be over emphasized. In fact, it may be preferable to omit the objective, rather than to put in something vague.

> **It is safer to omit the objective rather than insert a vague one.**

For example, the objective "To utilize my skills in a challenging position which will afford advancement and professional growth" tells the employer really nothing about you. The statement is too general to be of any value. Do not include an empty, "fluffy" objective. Either draft one that conveys useful information about you, and demonstrates that you know what the employer is looking for, or omit it altogether!

Guidelines for Your Objective

If you choose to include an objective, here are some guidelines. An objective may contain up to four parts. However, it is not essential that every objective has to contain all four. Just include as many parts as are applicable to the job

An objective may have as many as four parts.

Part one is the "level" of the position. Examples of position levels may be words such as "trainee", "temporary", "part-time", "fulltime", "entry level", "experienced", "supervisory" and "executive". If you know what level of position you are seeking, select one of the above terms, or create one of your own. In many cases, position level is not an important part of an objective, and can be left off.

Part two contains the skills you hope to use in that position. Refer to the list of skills given under "Build on Your Strengths" earlier in Chapter 4. This will help you to identify the job-relevant skills that you possess. For example, you may be seeking "A position in consulting, software design, development and support utilising my software, customer relations and problem-solving skills".

Part three is the position function, also sometimes called position title. If you are responding to a job posting, the position function can often be found in the text of the advertisement. Examples of functions are "chemist", "administrative assistant", "process engineer",

The position title is best picked up from the advertisement's text.

"accountant", "project manager", "consultant" etc. For those with broad skill sets, many position titles may apply. Find out what a specific employer calls this function within their organization from the advertisement or from an acquaintance working in that field. You may also choose to invent a title that is broad enough to encompass your unique vision.

Part four refers to the field or industry, in which you hope to work. You need to specify this in job applications that you may send without waiting for a formal job advertisement from a particular industry. Some of the examples of fields or industries include:

- Telecommunications.
- Higher education.
- Banking.
- Pharmaceuticals.
- Social services.
- Event planning.
- Resort/travel industry.

Your particular position may well be found in more than one field or industry. For example, accountants work in all of the industries listed above. If your career vision is not focused on any field or industry, then you may wish to omit this part of the objective.

Integrating all four parts into a cohesive whole is easy. The following objective contains all four parts. See if you can identify them.

"A full-time engineering position in the computer industry, which utilizes my ability to work as a team member and contributes to marketing, support, design and testing of products and services."

A sample objective with all four parts.

Employers expect that an applicant will customize his objective to suit each employer and each position for which a résumé is submitted. The days of creating one résumé and duplicating it 50 times are over. You can expect to require multiple versions of your résumé with customized objectives. The text of your résumé may also need to be modified, in both structure and content; to support the various customised versions.

The days of writing one résumé and duplicating it 50 times are over!

Examples

Here are just a couple of ways that others have communicated their objectives.

- Example #1 Entry-level

Objective

An entry-level position in your Quality Assurance Team

- Example #2 Mid-level

Career Objective

To combine my innovative marketing skills with knowledge of cutting edge technology as a member of a creative marketing team.

Hints:

If you have difficulty defining an objective for your résumé, you may wish to spend more time exploring your career or job goals. Perhaps, you need to think more about why you are writing a résumé. At times, it may be necessary to explore your interests, values and skills all over again and to gain more self-knowledge. It may also be necessary to explore the world of employment opportunities, as this scenario is quite dynamic. In short, you need to take a fresh look at your own skills and abilities on one hand, and the current job market on the other hand.

Review your career goals to draft a better objective statement.

Summary of Qualifications

This part of your résumé is sometimes called an "Executive Summary". It can be the most powerful section of your résumé. It is a brief statement of your experience, training and personal abilities. It can be expressed in one short paragraph or in bulleted format. Experts recommend that you should limit this to approximately six sentences or bulleted statements.

This part allows you to really talk about yourself in your résumé. It can summarize a breadth of experiences and call attention to skills not represented by your position titles.

It is especially useful when making a career change. Here, you want to immediately call the employer's attention to all the skills you have, not just those that are obvious in your job descriptions.

An executive summary is especially useful when making a career change.

Example

HRD Manager

Over 3 years' experience in developing, installing and administering a personnel training programme, that resulted in accelerated promotion of participating employees and reduced employee turnover by 30%.

Writing a summary can be quite a challenge. It requires you to think about your whole work life from a big picture perspective. Many times, people forget what they have done, if it happened some time ago, or have difficulty putting it into words.

Sometimes, you can jog your memory by looking at a list of action verbs so that you remember things you have done in the past. By searching through a list of verbs, you will not only remember your achievements, but you may also get some ideas for describing your past achievements in new ways. To get a start, you can look at the list of "key skills" under the section titled "Build on Your Strengths" in Chapter 4, earlier in this book.

List your "key skills" and use them to draft your executive summary.

However, this list is only a guide. You must prepare your own list of verbs. Try writing your own summary of qualifications using some of the skills. Keep in mind your job goal, and think about the key skills necessary to be successful in that area. Now, recalling your career/life experiences, which of those skills have you developed? The executive summary is also the right place to highlight your relevant personal strengths. While drafting the summary, think of characteristics such as being a team player, being exceptionally organized, being creative, artistic, or being detail-oriented.

Think also about the total number of years you have spent in your area of expertise; think about how well rounded your experience is.

Hints:

A useful exercise while preparing to write your summary of qualifications is talking aloud about your overall career and job skills and experiences. Be big-picture oriented and summary oriented. An employer can see who you have worked for and can see all the details about your experiences in the rest of your résumé. Now is your chance to help the employer understand how they all fit together.

Pull together themes and draw conclusions based on details you will provide later.

TIP

Sometimes, people find it easier to write this section after they have worked on the rest of their résumé. It is often helpful to go through the details of your skills and experiences, review them closely and then write the Summary of Qualifications at the end.

A close colleague you have worked with for a long time may be a good sounding board when you work on this section. Friends who are truly familiar with your work and work style are also good sources of assistance.

TIP

Keep in mind that what you include needs to be relevant to the job goal. Always be honest about the skills and experiences you mention but also be strategic. The more you know about the position and what the employer is looking for in an ideal candidate, the easier it is for you to search your job history and pull out the relevant strengths.

Guided Approach

Are you still having trouble with your executive summary on your own? Here's a guided approach to creating a professional summary. While we strongly encourage you to write your own summary, if you are completely stuck, then try out the procedure given below.

- #1. Select a heading for this section.

For example, write "Summary of Qualifications" or, "Executive Summary".

TIP

You can pick one of these headings, or others that may be more appropriate. The quality of your selection will depend on how thoroughly you review your own career and establish good matches between your skills and the job needs.

- # 2. Type a term you would use to describe what you do.

For example: Office Manager, Team Leader, or Scheduling Coordinator.

If you have held a variety of positions over the course of your career, what skills or responsibilities do they have in common? You could use such a common factor. For example, you could choose public speaker, office efficiency expert, computer trouble-shooter, etc. Here is another way to think about it. If you were to sell your services as part of your own business, what would you put underneath your name on your business card?

- #3. Take a look at your list of skills that you prepared while doing the key skill search exercise in Chapter 4. Note those skills that apply to most of your professional or work related experiences.

In your final skills list, pick one skill at a time and select from one up to six verbs that describe each skill. Select the verbs in which you have the most experience and expertise.

For the purpose of this exercise, make the verbs active by adding an "ing" at the end. Now type those action verbs (with the "ing" added) in the Verb box in the table below.

- #4. List the object on which the verb is acting. Type the objects in the "object boxes" next to the verb boxes in the table below.

Remember, the Action Verb (the action you do) is to be followed by Object (who or what you do it to)

Here is an example:

Sl #	**Action Verb**	**Object**
1	Counseling	First year students

- # 5. Fill in the table below, using as many action verbs as may be appropriate for the job you are applying for. Any number from 3 to 6 is appropriate. You would rarely wish to exceed 6. The sample is for only one skill. You can construct more tables.

Sl #	Action Verb	Object
1		
2		
3		
4		
5		
6		

Education

This section is designed to show an employer that you have the necessary educational credentials to do the job. Include in this section your traditional degrees and certificates as well as professional courses attended. It should show your academic breadth and intellectual accomplishments. It should even imply something about your industriousness and desire to improve yourself. Continuous learning is essential to remain competitive in today's job world and this section should show what you have done to stay up-to-date in your current field, and how you continue to do so. This section is of key importance if you are making a career change. Show here how your new or existing academic credentials can be related to the new career you are seeking.

Continuous learning is essential to remain competitive.

In addition to higher education degrees and certificates, also include all academic awards or scholarships and professional affiliations you have. Sometimes, it may also benefit you to include your marks obtained and/or rank in class.

Example

Education

B.Com, Delhi University, 1998
Main Subject: Economics
Subsidiary Subject: Mathematics
Overall Marks 78%
Class: First

A Suggested Approach

You can start this section by listing, in reverse chronological order, your college degree(s), the institution(s) you attended, the dates you received your diploma(s), and any academic honour(s) that you were awarded.

TIP

If you have attended professional courses towards a new degree or certificate or if you have taken training courses related to your new career goal, it is helpful to list them as well. If you have yet to complete a programme, or even if you have only applied for but haven't yet begun one, include the details! It will show your continuing commitment to improve yourself.

Hints:

Should you include your rank, class obtained and overall percentage? There is no hard-and-fast rule. Only include them if you think they will help to enhance your case. Marks obtained many years ago may no longer be an accurate reflection of just how good you are today. If so, then leave them out. Mention the name of the degree or certificate first if your degree directly applies to the job you are applying for. Otherwise, mention the name of the institution first, especially if the institution has a very high reputation in professional circles.

> **Marks obtained many years ago may not be an accurate reflection of just how good you are today.**

TRAP Consider the overall impact of all the entries you will show in the education section of your résumé before you decide. Remain consistent for all the entries. Do not change the order halfway down the list.

Now fill in the form below to complete the "education" section.

The Form

Higher Education Received

College	
Educational Institution	
City, State	
Degree/Diploma	
Main Subjects	
Additional Subjects	
Rank/Class/Marks%	
Graduation Date (Month/Year)	

List names of courses and optional brief descriptions that directly apply to your career or the job being applied for.

Related Training Programmes

Course	Description/Details

Include here details of additional formal courses that you may have attended.

Additional Professional Development Performance

Seminars/Workshops	Details of Course & Certificates

Provide details of relevant seminars or workshops attended, certificates received, etc. using the table above.

Notes:

1. In the forms shown above, the format has room to enter only one or two of your education or training details. This is only an example. Use as many rows and columns as you need.
2. Remember that education includes traditional academic learning and "hands-on" professional mini-

courses. You may include membership of relevant professional institutes or technical colleges as well (e.g. Indian Productivity Council courses, Indian Institute of Management programmes, membership of ICWA etc.)

Work Experience

This section assumes that you are writing a résumé in the reverse chronological order. If you decide that a functional format would be better for you, you can still use many of the things, you will learn from this section. The major difference is that you have to group your work experiences by job responsibility categories such as accounting skills, supervisory skills etc., as opposed to job titles such as Accountant, The Vanishing Chit Fund Company, or, Supervisor, The Collapsing Flyover Company, etc.

Your record of past work experience should clearly demonstrate your capability of doing the job you are now applying for.

Example

Experience

The Vanishing Chit Fund: **Senior Accountant**

1998 – present (promoted from Jr. Accountant)

- Managed team of 8 junior accountants including daily wok assignment and daily performance reviews.
- Successfully installed ORACLE based new accounting software two months ahead of schedule.
- Oversaw preparation of new departmental cost centre databases.

Pre-planning

Before you begin the work experience section, you will wish to decide a few things.

- What do you want to call this section? Here are just a few possibilities. Note the connotation that goes with each title.
    1. Work Experience (focuses attention on the quality of experiences you have had).
    2. Work History (focuses attention on the fact that you have worked for a significant period of time, hence, you have a "history").
    3. Professional Experience (suggests that the experiences you've had all required significant levels of professional education).
    4. Related Experience (suggests that you are not listing all of your work experiences, only those that are related to the position for which you are applying. Cover the rest under a separate heading titled "Other Experience").
- What jobs are you going to include?
    1. If this is not your first résumé, leave off part time jobs held during school or college unless they directly relate to the position for which you are applying.
    2. Leave out temporary jobs as long as there aren't large gaps in your work history. A large gap is more than 6 months.

3. Decide which is more important from the following. This information will be listed first in the work experience section of your résumé:

- Where you worked (your employer).
- Position Title (the job you held).

4. Select the one that strengthens your candidature more.

You are now ready to fill the form below that details your work experience. You will come across a format for a functional list of work experience amongst the sample résumé in Chapter 8.

The Form

Employer	Employer's Location (City, State)
Position Title	Dates of Employment (1/95 – 6/98 or, 1995 – 1998)
Activities	Action Verb Object Result

The "Activities" entry in the table above needs further explanation. Select action verbs that describe the activities you performed at each job. If you're currently in the position, add an "ing" onto the end of the verb (e.g., facilitating), otherwise put the words in the past tense (e.g., facilitated). Then, list the object on which the verb is acting followed by the result of the action.

You may refer to the list of action verbs earlier in this chapter, under the section on "Summary of Qualifications". See the sample below, written for a counselor working with first year college students.

Action Verb (The Action you do or did)	Counseling/counseled
Object (Who/What you do or did it to)	First year students
Result (How good you were at it)	58% got First class in the term end examination.

While you don't always have to fill in a result, employers love to learn not only what you did, but how much of it and how well! Quantifying the results is indeed an effective way to attract favourable attention.

Quantifying results is an effective way to attract favourable attention.

Depending on the job being described, you may select 3 or 4 action verbs applicable to that job. Usually, your most recent job should be covered in detail. For other jobs, just one or two action verbs will usually suffice.

Activities/Interests

An "Activities/Interest" section in your résumé is optional. Here are some reasons why you might decide to include it in your résumé:

- To demonstrate that you are a well-rounded person who has more dimensions than just work.
- To point out skills that has been demonstrated in your non-professional life.

- To account for gaps in employment.
- As an interest generator (possibly the employer shares, or is intrigued by your interest).

While they sound similar, activities and interests are actually different things. Activities are structured, as with clubs, professional associations, etc. Examples would be Member of Computer Club, President of Alumni Association, Member of Resident's Society, Red Cross Volunteer, etc. When you list activities, indicate the name of the organization, your role (e.g. member, volunteer, office held), and years of participation. For example: "Member, Computer Club of India, 1992 - 1995".

Although similar, activities and interests are actually different things.

Interests, on the other hand, are unstructured individual pursuits. Examples would be reading, cross-country jogging, sewing, photography, tennis, etc. When listing interests, usually (but not always) your role is obvious, requiring no mention, and years are not relevant.

TRAP When you choose to include activities and interests on your résumé, be aware that there are some activities or interests to which certain employers may have a strong positive or negative reaction. Anything, which indicates a religious or political affiliation, or a position on a controversial political issue, should perhaps be avoided, or inserted with full knowledge of the likely consequences.

Example

There are a variety of different headings that you can use for this section. Two of them are illustrated below.

Volunteer Activities

General Secretary, Student's Gymkhana, Indian Institute of Technology, Kharagpur 1990-1991

Activities/Interests:

- Member, Indian Photographic Society, 1995 – present.
- Correspondent, "Mid Week", Mumbai, 1998 -2000.
- Honorary Treasurer, Resident's Association, 1997-98.

In this chapter, we have walked you through a complete résumé writing exercise, beginning from the "Objective" statement right up to the "Activities/Interest" section. The thoughts and skills you have learned here should see you through almost any résumé writing task that you may encounter. For some examples of résumé written using these techniques, see Chapter 9, "Sample Résumé".

You must recognize, however, that the product so far will only be a rough draft. You will have the raw materials assembled, but not the finished product. In order to evaluate what you have written so that you can determine exactly what parts of your draft résumé needs more work; read the next chapter, Chapter 6 "Rate Your Résumé".

❑❑❑

6. Rate Your Résumé

The résumé is a statement about you, written by you. Obviously, a special effort will be needed to make an objective self-assessment! The modest amongst you will be too reticent, not laying claim to credit really due to you. The less inhibited may go too far; making claims that could be difficult to uphold during the interview.

It is difficult to be objective about your own résumé!

There is need therefore, to pause now that the first draft is ready. After the first flush of creative energy, there is need for reflection and systematic, objective evaluation so that the rough edges can be smoothed and the entire product can be polished till it shines. The revision is often far more difficult than the drafting itself. You may use the following techniques for an objective self-evaluation. As an additional input, recruit an experienced and trusted friend to critique your résumé if you can.

You be the Judge

The résumé needs to be strong and concise. The objective should clearly state your career goals while the body of the résumé should support the objective logically. Your résumé makes a personal statement about you and your career. It is a written down snapshot of your work, education and your professional life. It is important that you feel comfortable with your résumé's format and content. If the final product doesn't make you feel proud to use it as your personal sales tool, take time to make the changes necessary to achieve this goal.

The résumé is a written snapshot of your work, education and professional life.

Use the two evaluation forms given in the next section of this chapter to check your résumé. The résumé critique form covers:

1. Overall Appearance.
2. Specific Attributes.

Under each of these two main factors are several sub-factors. Rate each sub-factor as one of the following:

1. Accept.
2. Rework.

There is no need to use more gradations such as a scale of 1 to 5. Either the portion under review is okay as it is or, it needs more work. There is no middle ground!

The Critique Form

Critique your résumé in two parts, overall appearance and specific attributes.The critique form is in two parts. The first part deals with overall appearance and the second with specific attributes. The first part addresses the structure and the appearance of the résumé. The second part evaluates the résumé's actual contents. Evaluate each part on its own merits. That is, do not let the contents influence the evaluation of the appearance, or, appearance influence the evaluation of the contents. Give a break of a day or two between the initial drafting and the critique of your résumé to bring to bear the objectivity you will need.

Critique your résumé in two parts, overall appearance and specific attributes.

Multiple Evaluations

If possible, hand out a copy of your draft résumé and a set of evaluation forms to one or two trusted friends.

If you compare their evaluation forms with your own, you will get more than one dependable input to help you edit and polish your masterpiece. Having your friends use structured evaluation forms will yield much more useful information than just a quick overall feedback which may merely say "excellent" or "okay".

Overall Appearance	Accept	Rework
Is the layout pleasing to the eye?		
Does the written matter fit comfortably on the page without overcrowding or too much white space?		

Overall Appearance	Accept	Rework
Is the résumé on good quality bond paper and the typing clear and un-smudged?		
Is the résumé easily readable? (Bullets used, no long sentences, no obscure fonts, no abbreviations)		
Does the résumé use bold, italics and underlining to highlight strengths?		
Is important information located prominently at the left and near top of the page whenever possible?		
Overall rating for Appearance		

Assuming that the résumé passes the appearance test, let us look at it once again from the point of view of the quality of specific attributes.

Overall Appearance	Accept	Rework
Goal Focused: Does the text support the objective?		
Length: Can it be shortened? Is a page comfortably filled?		
Relevance: Is the material relevant and sequenced in order of importance?		

Overall Appearance	Accept	Rework
Format: Is the format (Chronological, functional, combination) appropriate for the most favourable presentation?		
Action Orientation: Do sentences and paragraphs begin with action verbs?		
Specificity: Does the résumé avoid generality and focus on specific performance and achievements?		
Completeness: Are all relevant information included?		
Bottom Line: How well does the résumé accomplish the ultimate purpose of getting the employer to want to interview the applicant?		
Quantified Results: Are the results of your past work experience quantified as far as possible?		

If any of the criteria gets a rework rating in any of the two parts, do go through your résumé once again, even if the overall ratings for appearance and/or attributes are acceptable. Pay particular attention to the deficient criterion this time around.

Armed with these two forms, filled in by yourself and one or two trusted friends, you should now have all the inputs you need to produce a masterpiece of a résumé.

TRAP

While we encourage you to get independent evaluations from friends, and to look at these evaluations objectively, it is good to remember that it is your résumé and their advice should be acted on only if you are convinced that by doing so, you will indeed improve on your résumé! So, base your corrective action primarily on your self-evaluation and use the friendly critiques as secondary inputs.

The end of Chapter 6 may be a good time to pause and review the contents of this book. You should now have all the tools you need to professionally plan, draft, format and review your résumé. By following these steps, you will surely produce a masterpiece that was so long hidden inside you, waiting for the right inspiration; to come out and impress the world!

❑❑❑

7. Electronic Résumé

The New Frontier

Increasingly, jobs are being advertised on the Internet. It is not uncommon to find an application form on the web page of a company seeking employees. You can download, fill in and post your résumé, or even fill in the form on-line and submit it for scrutiny.

Currently, these advertisements are mainly for information technology professionals. All employers do not yet have web pages. However, the scene is changing fast. Non-IT jobs too are likely to be advertised in this manner soon as more and more organizations set up their own websites, be it for advertisement, E-commerce or for any other reason.

How does this trend affect you? As a job seeker, you should be aware of the rather special characteristics of Internet ready résumé. Apart from the need to be concise, the formatting of your résumé must undergo a change.

A computer selects résumé using a different set of rules.

Increasingly, computers are being used for preliminary screening of electronically submitted résumé before human beings see the selected ones. Unlike humans, computers work on a different set of rules for selecting eligible candidates. Your electronic résumé must take this into account. We look at the specifics of impressing a computer in the sections that follow.

Computer-Friendly Résumé Tips

What job hunters of the new millennium need to know is that computers read résumé differently than people do. If you are applying to employers in the United States, this factor is already quite important. It will become so in India in course of time.

TRAP Those who do not know this fact risk having their résumé crash and burn in the embers of the electronic age. How big is the risk? Studies do not agree, but about half of all mid-sized companies and virtually all the giants in the US are already using job computers, to scan résumé by the thousands and store their data for instant recall. Growing numbers of third-party recruiting firms and state public employment services in the Western world are also turning to this method to initially screen the résumé they receive.

You can protect your résumé from becoming a casualty of computer-friendly fire by following these suggestions:

Focus on Nouns, not Verbs

The computer searches résumé for the "key words" it has been programmed to find. These are different from the action words that attract the attention of a human reading your résumé. This is because the computer does a "blind search" by counting certain key words (which are nouns) and selecting those résumé that contain a sufficient number of such key words. On the other hand, a human will evaluate your résumé by reading complete sentences and understanding the meaning. Hence, a human will use action words (which are verbs) found in your résumé as a guide. As you can see, the two systems work quite differently! The key words for an accountant, for example, might include "BCom accounting, accounts payable, accounts receivable, IT Amendments, and CA." If your scanned résumé doesn't contain these key words, the computer passes it by, and you are a dead duck!

Computers count nouns, humans look for action verbs.

TRAP While there are no absolute content rules in computer résumé searches, the majority of experts agree that the action verbs that work so well on paper résumé lose their punch on scanned and computer-screened résumé. Job computers rarely search for a match on verbs like "inspired, built, calibrated, represented, or verified." While your résumé should include action verbs for sentence flow and human eyes, a computer just will not search for them.

Use More Key Words

The answer is to use more key words. The higher the numbers of key words you have in your résumé the greater are your chances of leaving E-storage and popping up on the screen where humans can get a good look at you. The key words work as a kind of electronic bait to catch the computer's attention.

TIP

You have probably been advised by career counselors to seek trainee positions and acquire other work experiences, and to join student chapters of professional associations. They are right for many reasons; the newest is that such activities produce computer-recognised key words, improving the chances of your résumé being selected by a screening computer.

Strike a Balance

As time goes by and more and more companies induct computers for preliminary résumé screening, you will need to make your application computer-friendly, using some of the tips given here.

This is especially true if you apply to an overseas employer either by E-mail, or by filling in an on-line electronic application form. In either case, there is a very good chance that the preliminary screening will be entrusted to a computer.

However, after your résumé has survived the combat with the computer, it will be exposed to human scrutiny. Therefore, all that we have discussed in the first 7 chapters of this book will still apply. So, you have to strike a balance between action verbs for humans and key words (nouns) for computers! Whoever said that writing a masterpiece was easy?

8. Bonus Section

We shall now journey beyond résumé. This book is designed to hold your hand until you have written a winning résumé that assures you of an interview call. However, you, dear readers would surely not like to stop there. Your target is the job itself, not just a date with the interview board!

Although the tools and techniques for preparing for interviews, putting together portfolios and conducting salary negotiations will require a full sized book to do them justice, we enclose a few hints and tips on the vital issue of job search methods. We add this as a bonus to reward you for your patience in reading through this book. After all, job search is vital. It comes before even résumé writing!

Job Search Methods

More than three quarters of the employers, the world over do not advertise job openings. Instead they hire people they know or people who find out about the opening through word-of-mouth!

TIP

According to surveys, networking and direct contact with employer are the most effective job search methods. More traditional methods such as advertisements and employment agencies are less effective.

Networking

Develop and use your own network! Tell your friends, relatives and acquaintances that you are looking for a job and ask them if they know anybody looking for an employee with your skills and qualifications. And even if they do not know right away, ask them to keep you in mind in case they hear about any job openings that could be of interest to you. Tell them about your skills and experience, but even better - give them your résumé so that they remember your request.

Think of any other people who could be helpful! Maybe the person you sat next to in the 12th standard is now an IT director of a small but rapidly developing Software Company. Do not feel embarrassed to contact him and ask for any lead!

Join professional associations and attend meetings to get to know more people in your area of specialty.

The larger the number of people you contact, the quicker you will get a job!

Do remember that the larger the number of people you contact, the quicker you will get a job!

Direct Contact

Direct contact with an employer does take more courage, but is a very effective job search method. Call the employer directly! Find the name of the person who is most likely to be your boss if you get the job.

Prepare a 3-minute presentation for the preliminary interaction. In the presentation, tell the employer:

- What you are looking for (e.g. I am interested in a position of a software developer),
- About your experience and skills (I have 4 years experience in web page design),
- What have you achieved in your previous positions (I have designed over 20 web pages, for example, for *www.netware.com*, *www.arthurandersen.com* etc.),
- Ask if you can come for an interview.

Do not feel embarrassed if he replies that there are no positions open. Say that you would like to come and talk about future openings. If he says no, ask if he knows of someone who might need an employee with your skills and experience.

Direct Mail

Make a list of the companies you would like to work for. Find out who in their organization is most likely to become your boss if you get the job and send a résumé and covering letter to that person.

If there is no opening for a person with your skills and experience, the employer is very likely to forget about you. Take the initiative in your hands. Do not leave the next step to the employer; state in your covering letter that you will contact him and really do so!

Advertisements

Review business newspapers and professional magazines to locate a suitable position. Read articles about the companies that could be your potential employers. Do not hesitate to send your résumé and covering letter if you see news about expansion or diversification since they will need more people!

Use the Internet as a job search tool. Review the advertisements on company web pages and also search the on-line employment databases often. However, remember that Internet advertisements are seen by thousands of people, so competition for the advertised jobs is fierce. We encourage you to rely on other job search methods also, unless you believe that your qualifications are really superior. The Internet, however, is perhaps the best source of information of overseas job openings.

Use the Internet as a job search tool.

Government Employment Agencies

Government Employment Agencies offer their services for free. However, less than 10 per cent of all available job openings are known to these agencies and less than 5 per cent of all job seekers find jobs through them. Beyond entry-level jobs, such agencies offer very limited opportunities.

Private Employment Agencies

Private employment agencies are better at finding available positions for job seekers. They usually charge a fee to you or your potential employer. This fee may be quite high. However, if your need is urgent, this is indeed a good way to locate a suitable job quickly.

A Few More Tips

- Usually, private employment agencies learn about the job openings by phoning up companies that may need employees with your skills and experience. You can do it yourself! In addition to saving several hundred rupees, you will get experience that you can use in your next job search, or, you may start an agency yourself!
- Contact more than one employment agency, as it will significantly increase the number of potential organizations that will be contacted by them. Remember that employment agencies usually have several hundred job seekers. Therefore, be sure to follow up after you have registered with them.
- The job search process is a tough and time-consuming one. Do not get discouraged if you do not get a job as fast as you have hoped to.
- Most job seekers spend less than 10 hours a week actively looking for a job. If you are unemployed, spend at least 30 hours per week, job hunting. Schedule your day and keep to the schedule.
- Do remember to send thank you notes to all the people who have helped you in the search process. You may need their help the next time you are again in the job market!

TIP

Sometimes you cannot get a job simply because you do not have relevant education or training, experience or skills. If that is the case, do not get discouraged. Take training courses. Consider apprenticeship work that will supply you with the relevant work experience.

In Conclusion

We wish you luck! We are confident that mainly through your own efforts, and perhaps, with some small assistance from this book, you will land that job of your dreams! Go for it!

❑❑❑

9. Sample Résumé

Throughout this book, we have referred to three basic types of résumé: **chronological, functional** and **combined.** You have already seen several fragments of résumé in different chapters that either illustrate certain principles of résumé writing or demonstrate different résumé styles. However, to get the full flavour of the three distinct styles and to appreciate the difference in content between entry-level, mid-level and top-level applicants, it is necessary to look at some complete résumé. We do so, in this chapter.

Chronological Résumé

Résumé No. 1 – Personnel Manager

Bidesh Bose

18 Rose Villa, Eduljee Road
Cherai, Thane 400 601
Phone: 624 1243 Email: bose@hotmail.com

Objective

To apply my specialized knowledge and skills in personnel management and conflict resolution in a fast growing organization requiring skills in negotiations with labour unions.

Relevant Experience

1998- present: Assistant Personnel Manager, handling union negotiations, canteen management and grievance procedures for over 500 workmen in M/s Johnson & Co.

1996-1997: Management Trainee in Personnel Dept., responsible for setting up grievance procedure and employee state insurance scheme record keeping in M/s Johnson & Co.

Education

1996	Bombay University	M.Com	First Class
1994	Bombay University	B.Com	First Class

Scholarships/Awards

1996	Daxina Fellowship	Bombay U	M.Com Part I & II

Relevant Co-Curricular Activities

1994-1995	President, Student's Union, Podar College Bombay
1995	Winner, Inter-college debate organised by St. Xavier's College, Bombay

References

References will be made available on request.

Notes

- This is almost an entry-level résumé, written in the chronological style, but grouped for emphasis and underlined for correct impact. For instance, under "Experience", the nature of work done when he was a trainee has been underlined. However, the job title has been underlined when he was promoted to Assistant Personnel Manager.
- Note the use of the word "relevant" while referring to both experience and co-curricular activities. It implies that there is more, but it has not been reproduced here since it is not relevant to his objective.
- While writing the actual résumé, additional formatting should be used such as tables with borders, to set off the data under education, experience, co-curricular activities, etc. Choose a font and font size so that the whole résumé fits comfortably on one 8½ by 11 inch page.

Functional Résumé

Résumé No. 2 – Export Manager

Gourav Narang
C 9991 Udyog Vihar
Gurgaon, Haryana 122019
Tel: 0124 636 6991 Email: gnarang@vsnl.com

- - - - - - - - - - - Objective - - - - - - - - - - -

To find a challenging position as an Export Manager/ Commodity Trader for a rapidly growing organization with global reach where I can utilize my operational and direction setting strengths to produce time bound, exceptional results.

- - - - - - - Relevant Experience - - - - - - -

Export Management-Assistant Export Manager (1999-)

- Managed International business of $ 28.0 million in 2 years in sugar and wheat around the world, exceeding profitability target of 5%.

Recruited trained and managed a team of 5 who set up export branch in Africa. Team exceeded sales target by 30% in second year.

Commodity Trading - Trader, Coffee Desk (1995-1998)

- Traded in soft commodities, grains and vegetable oils for India's largest trading house. Increased sales averaging at 25% per annum over 3 years.

- Set up warehouse receipt based collateral commodity financing with major European bank at lowest rates in history of company.
- Set up trading in Coffee Futures Exchange of India

------ **Relevant Milestones** -------

Conceptualized, developed and installed a computerized cargo monitoring system, covering international ports, with provision to automatically adjust invoicing for exchange rate fluctuations by downloading latest rates from the Internet – (1997)

Headed team that developed computerized system for managing the foreign exchange exposure (over $700 million per annum) of the group of companies with automatic circuit breaker facilities for the group's risk management operations – (1998-2000)

---------- **Education** ----------

Indian Institute of Foreign Trade, MBA in International Business Management, 1995

Bombay University, Ruia College, B.Com., First Class, 1993

------ **Other Achievements** ------

Regular contributor to Knight Ridder, Economic Times and Financial Express

Panelist for publication of Indian Exporter's handbook

Notes

- This is a mid-level résumé in the functional style where experience has been grouped together by function (Export Management and Commodity Trading) rather than being presented chronologically. In fact, the higher-level job, that of export management has been shown first, though it has occurred later in the candidate's life.
- Note how the top half of the résumé contains the objective statement and the most significant work experience of the candidate. The reader must be hooked into reading the rest of the résumé by the time he has finished reading the top half of the first page.
- Underlining has been used judiciously so that the reader may not miss the points the candidate wants to stress even while skimming rapidly through the résumé.
- Results and achievements are quantified as far as possible. Nothing speaks louder than figures!
- Note the use of the word "relevant" while referring to both Experience and to Milestones. It implies that there is more, but it has not been reproduced here since it is not relevant to his objective.

Combined Résumé

- The depth and breadth of knowledge and experience of this senior level candidate requires more than one page.
- Observe, however, how the real heart of this candidate's superior performance and ability is condensed within the top half of the first page.
- The format is a mixture of functional grouping and reverse chronology to showcase the accomplishments and potential of the candidate adequately.
- Performance is quantified as far as it is possible to heighten the impact of important accomplishments. Underlining has been used to aid reading.

Résumé No. 3 – Chief Executive, Engineering Industry

Ganesh Mahadevan

36 B Poes Gardens
Sterling Road, Nugambakkam
MADRAS 600 001
Phone : 440 4321 Email: ganeshm@yahoo.com

Objective

To lead a profit center as CEO, in the engineering industry by inspired leadership and vision so as to double its turnover over the next five years, attaining an industry dominant position in quality and price competitiveness.

Repertoire of Relevant Skills

As Vice-President, Operations; turned around Indian Forgings, Mumbai, from loss to (average) 15% Operating Profits in 3 years, negotiating a new incentive agreement with the workmen, ending in 1999.

As General Manager Works, increased turnover of Maruti Iron and Steel, Sholapur, from Rs. 20 Crores to Rs. 60 Crores p. a. in 3½ years ending in 1996.

As Project Manager, implemented the Rs. 35 Crores joint venture BT-Fison insecticides plant at Thane, Maharashtra, with no cost overrun, 3 months ahead of schedule, attaining full production capacity in 6½ months, 1½ month ahead of schedule, between 1993 and 1995.

Intellectual Attainment

Harvard Business School, USA, MBA, Cum Laude 1990

Indian Institute of Technology, Madras, B Tech (Hons.) 1988

Madras University, (7th rank in State) B Sc 1984

Selected Professional Accomplishments

Associate Member, American Society of Mechanical Engineers

Associate Member, Institute of Engineers India

Panel member, Industrial Advisory Committee, Government of Tamil Nadu, 1998 – present.

Visiting Faculty, Department of Mechanical Engineering, Indian Institute of Technology, Madras, 1999-2000

Relevant Strength Areas

Problem Solving Skills as demonstrated by de-bottlenecking continuous casting plant at Maruti Iron and Steel, increasing output by 100 tonnes per annum (1993-1994)

Goal Setting Skills as demonstrated in setting and achieving departmental cost reduction goals at 20% per annum on an average, instrumental in the financial turn around of Indian Forgings (1997-1999)

Team Building Skills as demonstrated by forming, leading and performance monitoring of a performance enhancement task force in Indian Iron and Steel, instrumental in tripling output and sales in 3½ years (1992-1996)

Leading and co-coordinating skills as demonstrated by setting up Industrial Engineering department and guiding them to introduce the highly successful incentive scheme for the Indian Forgings factory that led to the company's turnaround. (1996-1997)

Liaison Skills as demonstrated in negotiating and obtaining industrial license as well as all local licenses and permits for setting up and operating the BT-Fison plant (1993)

International Résumé

The Indian economy has opened up to the world. Jobs in the fields of Information Technology and in many other areas beckon the adventurous to many distant shores.

Today's young Indian professionals need no longer to restrict their job search to this country alone. The whole world is in your grasp if you have as the Americans say, "Got what it takes!"

Résumé writing abroad, is a fine art. It is quite different from the résumé written in India.

To compete with foreign candidates on equal terms, it is necessary to get a flavour of how résumé are written in other lands (particularly, the USA and UK).

> **This book contains tips and tricks comparable to the best and latest in international résumé writing manuals.**

In preparing this book, we have taken the best and the latest from many lands. By the time you reach this point in the book, you would have the latest tools and techniques in your hand.

You are indeed ready now to create a masterpiece, fit for any international employer. However, a few samples, of overseas résumé, unchanged and reproduced "as is" will surely be of interest to you.

With this intent, we provide in the following pages, two typical résumé from the United States. Please keep in mind the unavoidable distortion to the format of the résumé as they are being reproduced in the smaller pages of this book instead of the normal 8½ by 11 inch page size.

Pay particular attention to the manner in which information has been organized and emphasized. How assertions are made, and backed up with actual attainment and performance data. In short, you will see how the principles we have discussed so far, have been put to good use.

Résumé # 4: Management Position, Financial Services
[Reverse Chronological Format]

MICHAEL BROWN
13 Meadow Street
Houston, Texas 77034
709-431 4314michael.brown@msn.com

OBJECTIVE

A challenging position in project management with a financial services organization that utilizes innovative technology to manage projects and initiatives.

SUMMARY

• Progressive project manager with broad-based achievements in commercial banking, financial planning, computer operations and problem solving.

• In-depth knowledge of the financial services sector.

• Effective planning and organizational skills.

• Ability to successfully manage multiple priorities and assignments

• Possess effective presentation, verbal and written communication skills.

• Proven capacity to approach problems effectively and creatively.

• Strong abilities to develop corporate strategy documentation.

- Articulate and creative, offering innovative and practical solutions.
- Able to direct and lead others to produce desired results.
- An experienced team player, bringing enthusiasm and energy into group efforts.

EXPERIENCE

CHASE MANHATTAN 1997- Present

Houston, Texas

Bank Operations Project Manager

- Develop and co-ordinate several bank's operations strategy documents that define corporate bank operations' directions and strategy for consolidations, mergers and acquisitions and implementing new technology.
- Perform project support with all levels of management, marketing, personnel and staff to co-ordinate bank operation projects, resolve problems, and communicate project status.
- Provide project management support for bank's operation projects for new and enhanced applications and system conversions.
- Perform supervisory and administrative functions for assigned staff of seven analysts.
- Promoted to Assistant Vice President in March 1999.

Branch Area Co-ordinator 1996-1997

• Monitored actual performance of branch office operations and financial market analysis.

• Analysed variances on a monthly basis, and formulated customized financial reports through the use of an in-house accounting system.

Senior Conversion & Procedures Analyst 1995-1996

• Reviewed, developed and documented standardized back office procedures and policies for bank's operations.

• Assisted in the planning of new and enhanced applications and products.

• Documented and standardized bank's operation practice models for the entire corporation.

HOME DEPOSIT 1993-1995

Houston, Texas

Assistant Manager

• Managed $15 million in deposits by providing a high level of knowledge of financial services and investments to our most sophisticated clientele.

• Developed and generated new, upscale customers and expanded existing customer base by providing premium services.

- Actively supervised the training of new employees.
- Responsible for investigating, researching and resolving all out of balance conditions within the branch.

EDUCATION AND TRAINING

University of Houston, Houston, Texas 1988-1993

MBA

- Focus on Financial Institutions

CFA Level II candidate

In-house training:

- Team management
- Role of distribution channels in today's banking environment
- What will be the key competitive advantage of tomorrow's leading retail banks
- Internet banking: how to benefit from it?

Résumé # 5: Computer Programmer
[Functional Format]

DANIEL MILES
15 Melrose Road Massachusetts, Massachusetts
523521(545) 432 9501
daniel.miles@oursolutions.com

JOB OBJECTIVE

Position in a rapidly growing software development company, which would best utilize my experience as a software developer and project manager.

PROGRAMMING SKILLS

Computers: IBM PC-compatible, UNIX Servers and Workstations

Operating Systems: UNIX, Linux, Solaris, Novell NetWare, Mac OS, MS Windows, MS-DOS Programming

Languages: Assembler, Fortran, Smalltalk-80, Smalltalk/V, Objective C, C++, C, Java, Perl, Python, Lisp, Scheme, Forth, Prolog, SAS, PL/1, Cobol Database Systems: SQL, ODBC, perlDBI, JDBC, DB/2, MySQL, PostgreSQL, DbVistaDocument Processing: TeX/LaTex, HTML, SGML, DSSSL, DocBook DTD, Jade DSSSL engine Version Control: RCS, CVS Web-Management: Apache, Apache-SSL, Perl, PHP/FI, PHP3, JSDK scripting Cryptography and Security: IPSEC, SSH, SSLeay, PGP2, TCP/IP firewalling

GUI Programming: Win16/Win32 API, Borland OWL 2.0, ParcPlace VisualWorks 2.0General UNIX administration

EXPERIENCE

OUR SOLUTIONS, Massachusetts, Massachusetts, 1997-to date

Project manager · Inventory and Materials Management and Cost Optimisation · Sales Order Processing System · Material Handling and Transportation Cost Optimisation · Warehousing System Layout

DATAHOUSE, Massachusetts, Massachusetts 1993-1997

Programmer · Production System Investigation · Job Shop Scheduling · Activities Based Time Planning System · Web Page Design · Inline Internet Software Store

EDUCATION AND TRAINING

B.Sc. in Information Systems Technology, University of Massachusetts, Massachusetts

Résumé # 6: Sales Professional
[Functional Format]

Casey Stanton

7509 Laredo Avenue, Austin, Texas 78741
512-555-8755-Casey@sprintmail.com

Automotive Sales Professional

- Highly motivated professional with a consistent track record of success in a competitive industry.
- Possess an effective combination of interpersonal/ sales/relationship-building skills and strong analytical and organizational abilities... resulting in thoroughly planned, well-executed marketing and sales strategies.
- Build and maintain loyal customer relationships based on trust & communication.

Key Areas of Expertise

- Sales and marketing of luxury automobiles
- Marketing campaigns
- Key account relationship-building and networking
- Product introductions
- Customer service and quality assurance
- Territory development
- Technical seminar/meeting/sales presentations
- Business analysis and planning

Experience and Achievements

ELITE MOTOR COMPANY, Dallas, Texas from 2000-2004

Sales Consultant

- Sold Mercedes-Benz automobiles with an average price of $55K, top price of $135K.
- Grew client base through positive, professional relationships with customers that led to repeat business and numerous referrals.
- Within 6 months, rose to #5 of 9 sales representatives.

ACURA OF DALLAS, Dallas, Texas from 1996-1999

Sales Representative

- Developing clients from a solid referral base and effective marketing strategies, sold Acura automobiles with an average price of $33K.
- Consistently ranked among top performers; #2 in 1998.
- Contributed to strong dealership statistics: #1 in sales out of 12 dealerships. in 6 cities.

SUN COUNTRY MERCEDES, Phoenix, Arizona from 1990-1996

Service Manager from 1995-96

- Selected by dealership owner for special assignment to improve the quality of service provided to our customers-a dealership priority in 1995. Brought a sales and service attitude to the department; reduced turnaround time and improved Customer Satisfaction Index by 8%.

Education

- BA Communications, 1995
- Texas Christian University, Fort Worth, Texas.
- Earned 100% of college tuition and expenses through employment and entrepreneurial ventures.

Note

Casey liked selling luxury automobiles and was good at it. She has a good professional experience which is her key strength though her educational qualification is not much.

Ignore, for a minute, the names of institutions and employers. Observe, instead the content and the style. Relate them to the Indian samples (# 1 to 3) that you have already seen. The similarity in style, format and content is easy to see.

❑❑❑

Unicorn Bestsellers

9376 C • ₹ 296/-

9703 C • ₹ 125/-

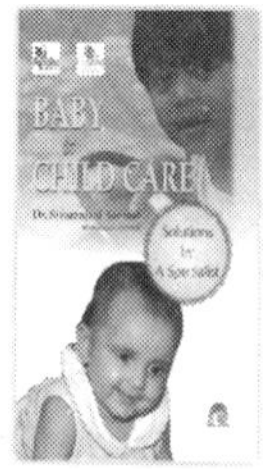

9717 K • ₹ 150/-

9336 B • ₹ 135/-

9376 B • ₹ 150/-

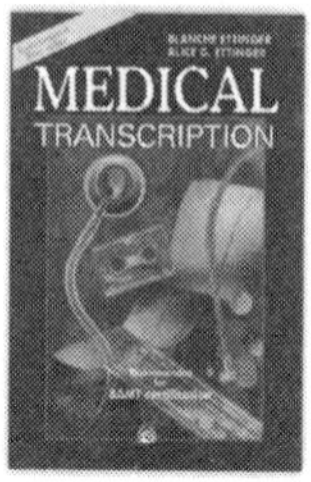

9207 D • ₹ 450/-

9351 D • ₹ 150/-

5625 D • ₹ 110/-

9272 A • ₹ 150/-

7795 E • ₹ 150/-

9324 E • ₹ 60/-

9369 D • ₹ 150/-

9213 F • ₹ 88/-

9333 D • ₹ 96/-

9355 D • ₹ 150/-

9971 C • ₹ 80/-

Job and Career

₹ 96/-

₹ 150/-

₹ 150/-

₹ 150/-

₹ 110/-

₹ 96/-

₹ 125/-

₹ 125/-

₹ 295/-

₹ 150/-

₹ 150/-

₹ 96/-